BUILD A TOWN
AND OTHER GREAT
LEGO® IDEAS

Contents

Book breakdown

This book shows lots of inspiring model breakdowns to help you discover ideas and techniques for your own models, but the entire book is broken down, too. There are many different types of pages designed to help you build up your own amazing LEGO® world, section by section, model by model, brick by brick.

Colored bars, like the one below, run along the top of pages to let you know what kind of page you're reading.

Page number   Page type

Section name

Here are all the different types of pages you'll find in this book:

How to build

Watch one model develop from start to finish on these pages, with helpful building advice at every stage.

What else can you build?

Once you've seen how to build one model, discover different ways of using similar techniques and ideas in your own models.

Model galleries

Little details can really help build up a scene. Check out these pages for a collection of smaller models you can make using a small number of bricks.

Expanding your world

Don't stop now! Once you've built a few models, why not add more to your world? These pages give ideas for building extra models and scenery.

Builder secrets

Ssshh! These pages reveal insider tips for building challenging parts of models or functions. Master the techniques to wow your friends!

A basic building

The city planner begins the construction of her new city with a single modular building. By following the same basic steps but changing the colors and details around, you can connect a few similar buildings together to make an entire city block.

> If you don't have these special 1x4 plates with two studs, you could use a smooth 1x2 tile with a studded 1x1 plate at each end instead.

START HERE

Always put these bricks with round holes in the same spots

1 > Starting out

On a large rectangular base plate or several smaller ones, start building a wall around three of the edges, leaving one long side open. Place four 1x2 bricks with holes on the sides, just like in the picture.

2 > Build up the walls

Build the three walls up to a height of six bricks, laying a long brick across the open side at the top. Add a layer of smooth tiles, with just four studs sticking up.

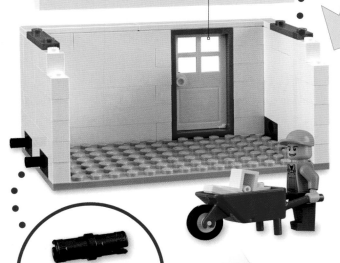

Use a LEGO door, or you could leave an open space

These round LEGO® Technic pins will let your building plug into the round holes of another building next to it.

This window is two bricks up from the base plate and fits in a space that is four studs across and three bricks high

3 > A second module

Now build a second building module, just like the first one...but instead of a door, build a window into the long wall at the front of the building.

Keep adding more stories, or put a plate on top as a roof

4 Building complete

With two modules, you've put together a great two-story building. Would you rather make it three stories tall, or even four? Just build more modules and stack them on top. You can make longer buildings, too, by joining the modules side-by-side.

The sturdiest walls have staggered rows of bricks just like real houses

A 1x1 round plate makes a good doorknob

ERM, I THINK WE FORGOT SOMETHING... STAIRS!

OOPS.

SIDE-BY-SIDE

Leave a door-shaped hole in these connecting walls to let your minifigures walk between the rooms

The modules connect side by side by snapping the LEGO Technic pins into the round holes at the base of the walls

With one door, these modules look like one long house. Add a door to the second module, and they're next-door neighbors!

Modular buildings

These buildings were all constructed in a modular style similar to the ones on the previous page. Stacking modules on top of each other creates office blocks and other tall buildings found all around town.

WHAT'S NEXT

Now you can expand your modular building technique by customizing the design with taller walls and extra architectural details.

OFFICE BLOCK

> *IT'S LONELY AT THE TOP.*

The company president gets the whole upper floor to himself

With modular building, you can add more floors as the company grows

1x6x5 panels let you build large sections of wall quickly. Use clear ones for big windows!

> *LANCE ALWAYS FORGETS MY SUGAR.*

The wall of the reception floor is stepped in to create an entrance with flower boxes

Office block

This modern office building looks organized and professional. Its modules appear similar from the outside, but on the inside each has its own particular function to keep the business running smoothly.

REAR VIEW

Look at pages 16–19 to see some of the furniture on these pages in more detail.

Library

This library is three modules high, with an extra rooftop section on top. Like the real thing, it has a checkout desk, a research room, and lots of books to borrow and read.

Keep track of the time with a printed 2x2 round clock tile attached to bricks with sideways-pointing studs

LEGO books don't attach to studs, so build shelves or storage racks to hold them

LIBRARY

Use slopes of differing heights and colors to make an angled rooftop

Alternate rows of regular and textured bricks, such as log bricks, create interestingly patterned walls

YEP, OLD NEWS IS THE BEST NEWS.

The windows stick out from the wall with the aid of 2x2 slopes above and 2x2 inverted slopes below

Book scanner is made from a sci-fi ray gun with a transparent red 1x1 tile on the end

REAR VIEW

City buildings

As the city planner's metropolis grows, more building shapes start to pop up. They might all be built around basic box shapes, but the colors, details, and piece selection make each of these city buildings unique.

WHAT'S NEXT?

Combining boxes in different ways means you can build in a variety of shapes, including making some more complex buildings.

CORNER SHOP

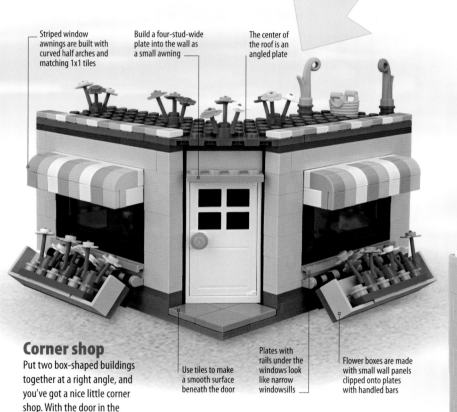

Striped window awnings are built with curved half arches and matching 1x1 tiles

Build a four-stud-wide plate into the wall as a small awning

The center of the roof is an angled plate

By making the walls two studs thick, you can set the windows back from the outside edge and strengthen the building's structure

Use tiles to make a smooth surface beneath the door

Plates with rails under the windows look like narrow windowsills

Flower boxes are made with small wall panels clipped onto plates with handled bars

Build a sidewalk in front with large tiles

Corner shop

Put two box-shaped buildings together at a right angle, and you've got a nice little corner shop. With the door in the middle and both sides matching, it looks like it's all one store.

Hospital

Combine multiple boxes into one building with
an unusual shape. A modern hospital has many
different sections, and each can be represented
by a box of a different shape and style.

A window at the back
adds more light inside

REAR VIEW

HOSPITAL

The smaller top floor is
set one stud back from
the ground floor

BONES? I ALWAYS THOUGHT I WAS HOLLOW INSIDE!

Feature window
The red section is the eye-catching center of the building.
Slopes and inverted slopes help to make an extra-big box
that sticks out beyond the edges
of the upper level.

Tall, thin windows
make a building look
important and longer
than it really is

Patients might drive up, walk
in, or arrive by ambulance,
so include several entrances

City museum

This ornate city museum is an example of how you can make a simple box-shaped building more exciting by adding interesting architecture. Check your collection for pieces with special shapes and textures.

Use clear slopes for skylight windows set into the museum roof.

Carvings are 1x1 round plates, bricks, and cones

Plates with rails for extra details

Square columns are stacks of 1x2 textured bricks

Use tooth plates for column decorations

I JUST LOVE LOOKING AT OLD BRICKS.

Classical architecture

Many of the details on this grand building are inspired by Classical Greek and Roman architecture. These include the columns at the front, the fancy portico over the doorway built from round bricks and cones, and the "frieze" around the sides made of bumpy log bricks.

Add a round tile for the door handles

Slopes and shiny tiles create white marble steps

An arch above the window for classic elegance

This ornate dragon window is found in LEGO® NINJAGO® sets

Portico columns made from 2x2 textured round bricks

NIGHT VIEW

Gallery of the past

Your museum will be even more believable if artifacts can be glimpsed through its windows. Create some mini-galleries inside!

Attach historical minifigure accessories to the wall with side-stud bricks

Use 1x2 transparent bricks to make display cases

The low wall is made from 1x10 plates, 1x1 cones, 1x1 round plates, and a layer of smooth tiles on top.

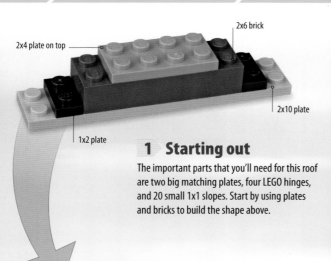

2x4 plate on top

2x6 brick

2x10 plate

1x2 plate

Building roofs

One of the city planner's favorite parts of a building is its roof. A roof can be simple or fancy, angled or flat. Here are two easy rooftop designs that you can use to top off your own metropolis models!

1 ▶ Starting out

The important parts that you'll need for this roof are two big matching plates, four LEGO hinges, and 20 small 1x1 slopes. Start by using plates and bricks to build the shape above.

2 ▶ Building up

Next, place the 1x1 slopes as shown. When properly arranged, they will form a bed to support the shape of the angled rooftop. If you don't have this many slopes in the same color, mix them up!

Put the hinges on the sides first, and then connect the roof plates

3 ▶ Final stage

Add the two-piece hinges so that they point in opposite directions. Attach the rooftop plates across two of these builds, and you're done!

Make sure you snap the hinges together the right way around

The flat part of the hinge is supported by a pair of 1x1 slopes from underneath

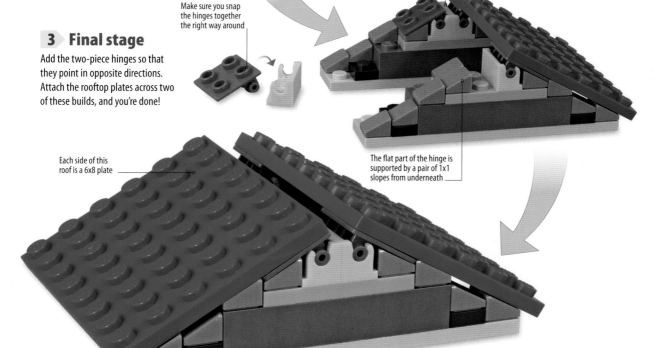

Each side of this roof is a 6x8 plate

COMPLETED ROOF 1

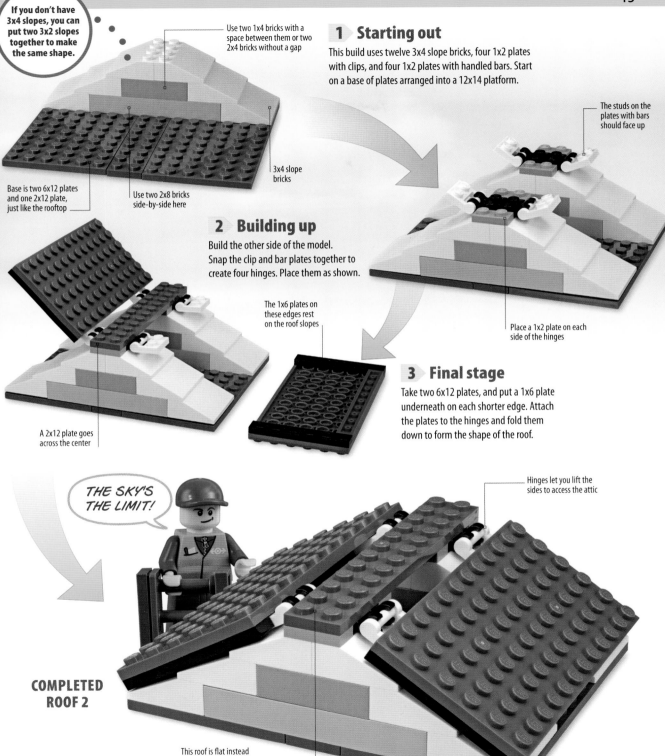

If you don't have 3x4 slopes, you can put two 3x2 slopes together to make the same shape.

Use two 1x4 bricks with a space between them or two 2x4 bricks without a gap

The studs on the plates with bars should face up

1 ▶ Starting out

This build uses twelve 3x4 slope bricks, four 1x2 plates with clips, and four 1x2 plates with handled bars. Start on a base of plates arranged into a 12x14 platform.

3x4 slope bricks

Base is two 6x12 plates and one 2x12 plate, just like the rooftop

Use two 2x8 bricks side-by-side here

2 ▶ Building up

Build the other side of the model. Snap the clip and bar plates together to create four hinges. Place them as shown.

The 1x6 plates on these edges rest on the roof slopes

Place a 1x2 plate on each side of the hinges

A 2x12 plate goes across the center

3 ▶ Final stage

Take two 6x12 plates, and put a 1x6 plate underneath on each shorter edge. Attach the plates to the hinges and fold them down to form the shape of the roof.

THE SKY'S THE LIMIT!

Hinges let you lift the sides to access the attic

COMPLETED ROOF 2

This roof is flat instead of peaked in the middle

Tables and chairs gallery

Without chairs, we would have to stand up all the time.... and think of how messy mealtimes would be without tables! Build some furniture to make your citizens' lives more comfortable.

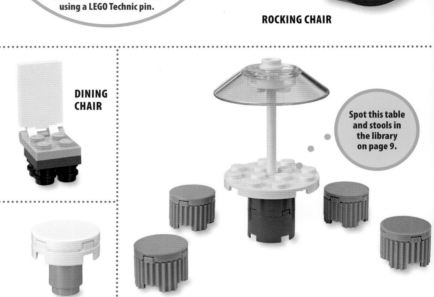

1x2 plate armrest

Pin fits into this 1x2 brick with hole

1x4 arch

The rocker and armrest on this rocking chair are built upside down and attach to the seat using a LEGO Technic pin.

THIS CHAIR ROCKS.

ROCKING CHAIR

DINING CHAIR

Spot this table and stools in the library on page 9.

STOOL

CAFÉ TABLE AND STOOLS

THANK GOODNESS FOR THIS QUIET CORNER.

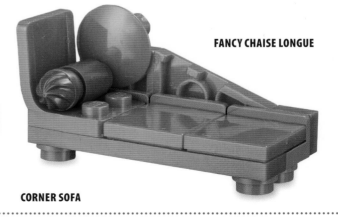

FANCY CHAISE LONGUE

CORNER SOFA

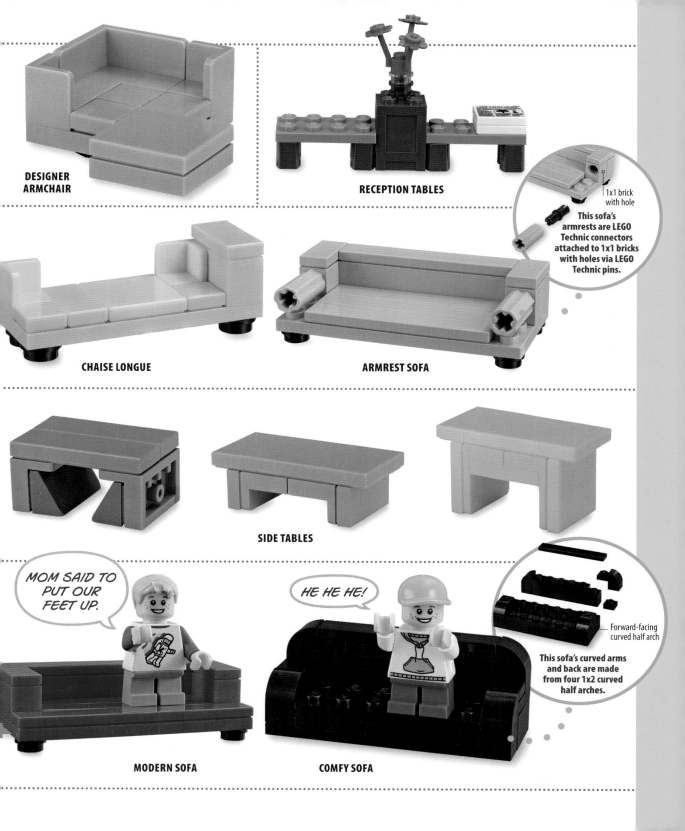

DESIGNER ARMCHAIR

RECEPTION TABLES

1x1 brick with hole

This sofa's armrests are LEGO Technic connectors attached to 1x1 bricks with holes via LEGO Technic pins.

CHAISE LONGUE

ARMREST SOFA

SIDE TABLES

MOM SAID TO PUT OUR FEET UP.

HE HE HE!

Forward-facing curved half arch

This sofa's curved arms and back are made from four 1x2 curved half arches.

MODERN SOFA

COMFY SOFA

Furniture gallery

Here's a collection of common and not-so-common objects from inside city buildings. Use these small but detailed builds to make your building interiors more lifelike and fun.

THIS ONE'S A GREAT READ!

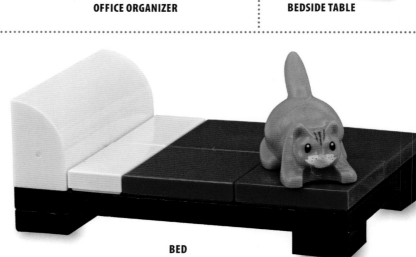

OFFICE ORGANIZER

BEDSIDE TABLE

BED

BOOKSTAND

BOOKSHELF

SHELF UNIT

COLORED LIGHTS

DESK LAMP

SOLAR LIGHT

ADJUSTABLE LAMP

See some of these models inside the buildings on pages 8 and 9.

I'LL SWAP YOU SOME FILES FOR A CROISSANT.

OFFICE DESKS AND FURNITURE

WATER COOLERS

FLATSCREEN TV

Around the city

What other models can you build to go outside the buildings and on the streets of your city? Here are some familiar sights that you'll be likely to find in any good metropolis.

ATM

Do your citizens need cash in a hurry? Place an automated teller machine against the side of a building, or build it directly into the wall.

This sign is held on by an angle plate, but you can use any piece with side studs.

Keypad is a 2x2 slope brick with a sticker attached

A 1x2 plate with rail keeps the money tile from going so far in that it gets stuck

Bike racks

How do you store a LEGO bicycle so that it doesn't block the sidewalk? These racks solve the same problem in two different creative ways.

This rack uses 1x2 plates with hook-shaped bars to suspend the bikes end-to-end at an angle

END-TO-END RACK

This version uses L-shaped bar elements plugged into side-stud bricks to prop the bikes up side-by-side

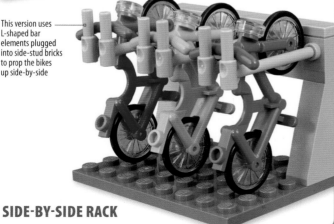

SIDE-BY-SIDE RACK

This headlight brick is filled out by a 1x1 plate.

Fire hydrants

All you need to build a fire hydrant are a 1x1 round brick, some 1x1 round plates, and a 1x1 brick with one or more side studs.

A 1x1 plate with clip holds the phone when it's not in use

The kiosk's phone details attach to the sideways-facing studs of an angle plate bracket built into the back of the model.

Kiosk "buttons" are a printed 1x2 tile

This phone booth has a door for privacy

...BUT WHERE ARE THE APPS?

THIS IS HOW WE USED TO TALK ON THE PHONE, TIMMY.

1x2x3 C-shaped windows in the middle make space for a minifigure's arms

Slopes at base support the wider top

KIOSK

Public telephones

In the days before cell phones, this is how people used to stay in touch when they weren't at home! A public telephone will add a little color to your city street. Here are two different ways to build one.

BOOTH

Puppet show

A puppet theater will keep your city's kids smiling. The puppets are minifigure heads fitted on the ends of flick-fire missile pieces!

Back of 1x1 side-stud bricks

YIKES!

GRRRRR.

Horns pushed into hollow side-stud bricks hold up the minifigure-cape curtain.

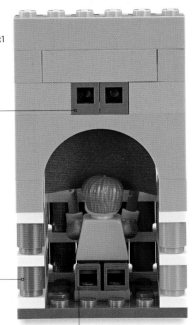

Base is a three-walled box made with plates and 1x1 round bricks

Turn minifigure legs around for a kneeling pose

REAR VIEW

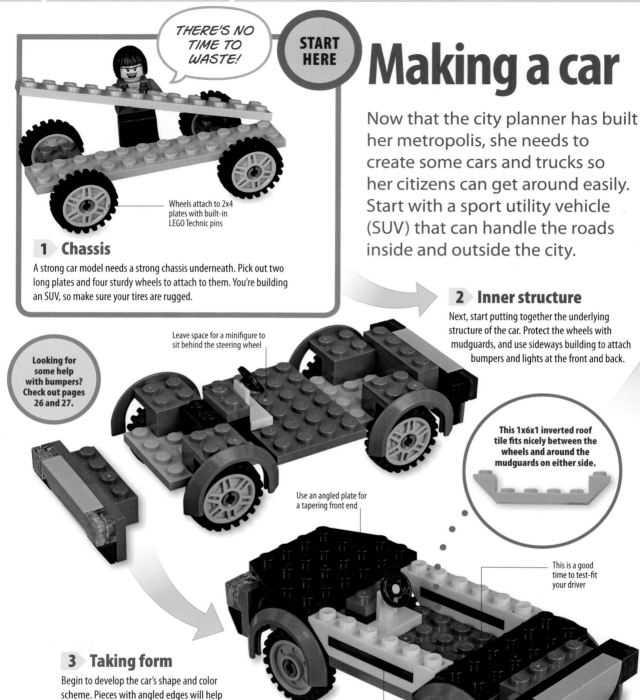

THERE'S NO TIME TO WASTE!

START HERE

Making a car

Now that the city planner has built her metropolis, she needs to create some cars and trucks so her citizens can get around easily. Start with a sport utility vehicle (SUV) that can handle the roads inside and outside the city.

Wheels attach to 2x4 plates with built-in LEGO Technic pins

1 ▶ Chassis

A strong car model needs a strong chassis underneath. Pick out two long plates and four sturdy wheels to attach to them. You're building an SUV, so make sure your tires are rugged.

2 ▶ Inner structure

Next, start putting together the underlying structure of the car. Protect the wheels with mudguards, and use sideways building to attach bumpers and lights at the front and back.

Leave space for a minifigure to sit behind the steering wheel

Looking for some help with bumpers? Check out pages 26 and 27.

This 1x6x1 inverted roof tile fits nicely between the wheels and around the mudguards on either side.

Use an angled plate for a tapering front end

This is a good time to test-fit your driver

3 ▶ Taking form

Begin to develop the car's shape and color scheme. Pieces with angled edges will help to keep it from looking too square and blocky. It's especially important to lock down the mudguards so they won't pop loose.

A sandwiched black plate creates a stripe on the side of the car

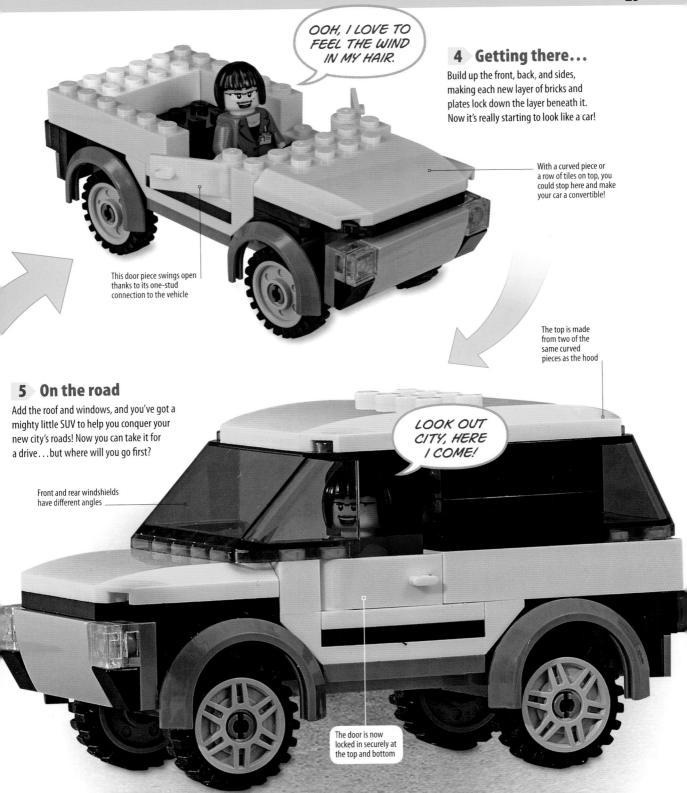

OOH, I LOVE TO FEEL THE WIND IN MY HAIR.

4 Getting there...

Build up the front, back, and sides, making each new layer of bricks and plates lock down the layer beneath it. Now it's really starting to look like a car!

With a curved piece or a row of tiles on top, you could stop here and make your car a convertible!

This door piece swings open thanks to its one-stud connection to the vehicle

The top is made from two of the same curved pieces as the hood

5 On the road

Add the roof and windows, and you've got a mighty little SUV to help you conquer your new city's roads! Now you can take it for a drive...but where will you go first?

Front and rear windshields have different angles

LOOK OUT CITY, HERE I COME!

The door is now locked in securely at the top and bottom

City vehicles

What vehicles will your metropolis need? How about an ambulance for a hospital (see pages 10–11) or a scooter to help people zip around town? You could make a bike taxi for anyone who doesn't like to cycle themselves.

AMBULANCE

WHAT'S NEXT?

Start your model with a basic chassis made from some plates and spinning wheels. Where you go from there is up to you!

Transparent colored plates make emergency flashers over the cab

FRONT VIEW

HA 3221

Ambulance

When your citizens are feeling poorly, the speedy ambulance is ready to whisk them off to the city hospital. Leave space inside for the patient and lots of medical equipment.

White with red accents is a recognizable color scheme for medical treatment

Side mirror is a 1x1 slope attached to a plate with a side ring

Headlights and taillights are 1x1 plates built directly into the vehicle

WE'LL HAVE YOU FEELING BETTER SOON.

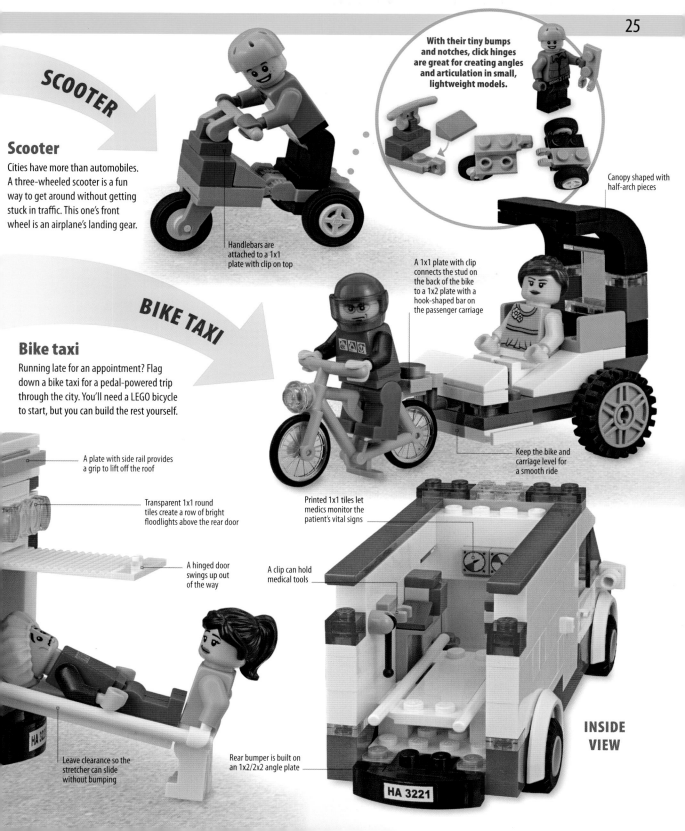

SCOOTER

Scooter

Cities have more than automobiles. A three-wheeled scooter is a fun way to get around without getting stuck in traffic. This one's front wheel is an airplane's landing gear.

With their tiny bumps and notches, click hinges are great for creating angles and articulation in small, lightweight models.

Canopy shaped with half-arch pieces

Handlebars are attached to a 1x1 plate with clip on top

A 1x1 plate with clip connects the stud on the back of the bike to a 1x2 plate with a hook-shaped bar on the passenger carriage

BIKE TAXI

Bike taxi

Running late for an appointment? Flag down a bike taxi for a pedal-powered trip through the city. You'll need a LEGO bicycle to start, but you can build the rest yourself.

Keep the bike and carriage level for a smooth ride

A plate with side rail provides a grip to lift off the roof

Printed 1x1 tiles let medics monitor the patient's vital signs

Transparent 1x1 round tiles create a row of bright floodlights above the rear door

A clip can hold medical tools

A hinged door swings up out of the way

Leave clearance so the stretcher can slide without bumping

Rear bumper is built on an 1x2/2x2 angle plate

INSIDE VIEW

HA 3221

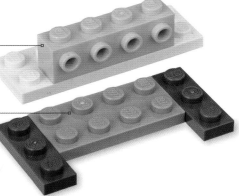

You could also use two 1x2 or four 1x1 bricks with side studs

These three plates are held together by the bigger plate on top

Auto bumpers

Believe it or not, bumpers can be the hardest part of a car or truck model to build. Try using these techniques to make your own detailed and good-looking auto bumpers.

1 ▶ Basic structure

Start by placing a 1x4 brick with side studs on a 2x6 plate with the studs pointing out. Add an under-layer made from a 2x4 plate and two 1x3 plates.

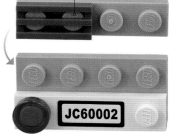

Attach two 1x2 LEGO grilles to a 1x4 plate

2 ▶ Build the details

The face of the bumper is built on a 2x4 plate. Assemble a grille for the top half, and a license plate area with side-lights for the bottom half.

JC60002

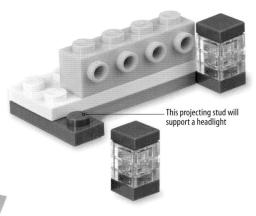

This projecting stud will support a headlight

3 ▶ Put it together

Make headlights by stacking up three transparent 1x1 plates with a 1x1 tile on top. Attach these on the sides. Next, connect the face to the side-stud brick to complete the bumper.

The license plate is a stickered piece from a LEGO fire truck

The round tiles could be red, yellow, or colorless transparent pieces

Combine square and round transparent plates for headlights and taillights

JC60002

COMPLETED BUMPER

OTHER BUMPER IDEAS

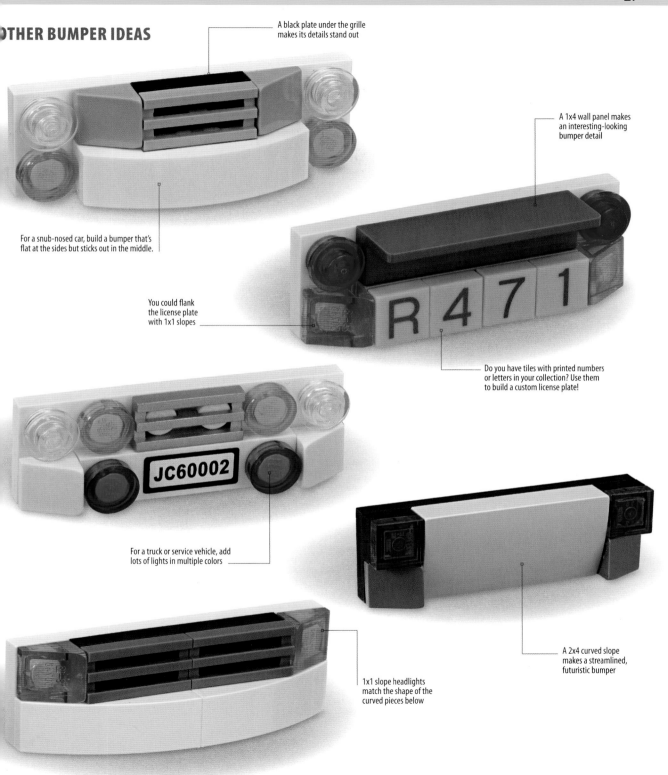

A black plate under the grille makes its details stand out

A 1x4 wall panel makes an interesting-looking bumper detail

For a snub-nosed car, build a bumper that's flat at the sides but sticks out in the middle.

You could flank the license plate with 1x1 slopes

Do you have tiles with printed numbers or letters in your collection? Use them to build a custom license plate!

For a truck or service vehicle, add lots of lights in multiple colors

A 2x4 curved slope makes a streamlined, futuristic bumper

1x1 slope headlights match the shape of the curved pieces below

Lights, signs, and signals gallery

What else does a road system need? Build streetlights, traffic signals, directional signs, and other accessories to keep your city's traffic flowing smoothly.

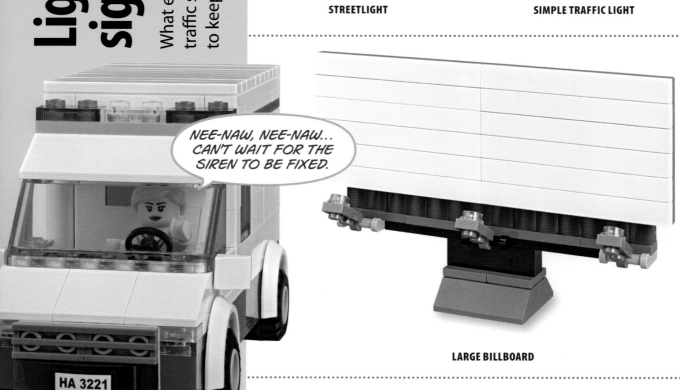

This useful bar-holder-with-clip element has a hole at one end and a clip at the other.

STREETLIGHT

SIMPLE TRAFFIC LIGHT

NEE-NAW, NEE-NAW... CAN'T WAIT FOR THE SIREN TO BE FIXED.

LARGE BILLBOARD

HA 3221

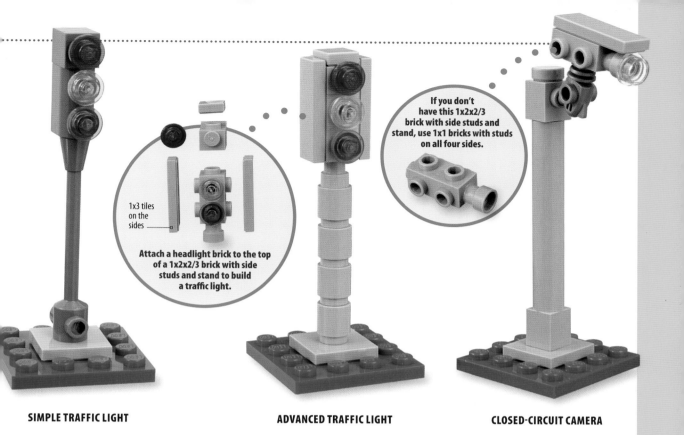

1x3 tiles on the sides

Attach a headlight brick to the top of a 1x2x2/3 brick with side studs and stand to build a traffic light.

If you don't have this 1x2x2/3 brick with side studs and stand, use 1x1 bricks with studs on all four sides.

SIMPLE TRAFFIC LIGHT

ADVANCED TRAFFIC LIGHT

CLOSED-CIRCUIT CAMERA

SMALL BILLBOARD

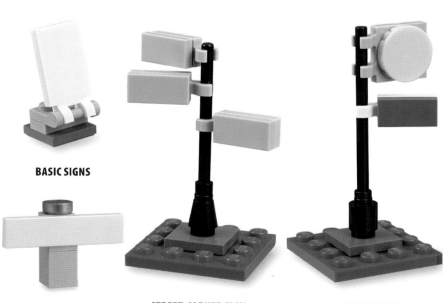

BASIC SIGNS

STREET-CORNER SIGN

TRAFFIC SIGN

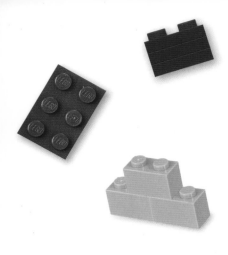

DK | Penguin Random House

Senior Editor Hannah Dolan
Editor Matt Jones
Editorial Coordinator Clare Millar
Senior Designers Mark Penfound, Lisa Sodeau
Project Art Editor Lauren Adams
Designer Thelma Jane Robb
Design Assistant Ellie Bilbow
Pre-Production Producer Kavita Varma
Senior Producer Lloyd Robertson
Managing Editor Paula Regan
Design Managers Jo Connor, Guy Harvey
Creative Manager Sarah Harland
Publisher Julie Ferris
Art Director Lisa Lanzarini
Publishing Director Simon Beecroft

Models built by Yvonne Doyle, Alice Finch, Rod Gillies, Tim Goddard,
Tim Johnson, Barney Main, Drew Maughan, and Pete Reid
Photography by Gary Ombler

Dorling Kindersley would like to thank Randi Sørensen, Henk van der Does, Melody Caddick,
Alexandra Martin, Heike Bornhausen, Paul Hansford, Robert Ekblom, and Lisbeth Finnemann
Skrumsager at the LEGO Group. Thanks also to Pamela Afram, Beth Davies, Andy Jones, Keifer
Lewin-Nation, and Scarlett O'Hara at DK for editorial assistance, and Jon Hall, Pamela Shiels,
Rhys Thomas, and Jade Wheaton for design assistance.

This edition published in 2018
First American Edition, 2017
Published in the United States by DK Publishing
345 Hudson Street, New York, New York 10014
DK, a Division of Penguin Random House LLC

Contains content previously published in LEGO® Awesome Ideas (2015)

Page design copyright © 2018 Dorling Kindersley Limited

002-308350-July/18

A catalog record for this book is available from the Library of Congress.

ISBN: 978-5-0010-1477-5

Printed in Guangdong, China

www.LEGO.com
www.dk.com

A WORLD OF IDEAS:
SEE ALL THERE IS TO KNOW